The ESSE

MW00990398

PASCAL I

Gary W. Wester, Ph.D.

This book covers the usual course outline of
PASCAL I. For related topics, see *"THE
ESSENTIALS OF PASCAL II"*.

Research and Education Association
61 Ethel Road West
Piscataway, New Jersey 08854

THE ESSENTIALS® OF PASCAL I

Revised Printing, 1994

Printed in the United States of America

Library of Congress Catalog Card Number 89-62090

International Standard Book Number 0–87891–694-6

WHAT "THE ESSENTIALS" WILL DO FOR YOU

This book is a review and study guide. It is comprehensive and it is concise.

It helps in preparing for exams, in doing homework, and remains a handy reference source at all times.

It condenses the vast amount of detail characteristic of the subject matter and summarizes the **essentials** of the field.

It will thus save hours of study and preparation time.

The book provides quick access to the important facts, principles, theorems, concepts, and equations in the field.

Materials needed for exams can be reviewed in summary form – eliminating the need to read and re-read many pages of textbook and class notes. The summaries will even tend to bring detail to mind that had been previously read or noted.

This "ESSENTIALS" book has been prepared by an expert in the field, and has been carefully reviewed to assure accuracy and maximum usefulness.

Dr. Max Fogiel
Program Director

CONTENTS

CHAPTER 1

BASIC PASCAL

1.1   PROGRAM STRUCTURE

The general structure of a Pascal program is illustrated in the following diagram:

program *prg-name (file-list);*

label
    { label section }
const
    { constant section }
type
    { type section }
var
    { variable section }

    { subprogram section }

begin
    { executable statements }
end.

The general structure of a Pascal program may be divided into three parts: program heading, declaration part, and statement part.

1.1.1 PROGRAM HEADING

The first statement in a Pascal program is the program heading. This statement gives the program name and the kinds of input/output operations that will be performed by the program. The program heading is required for Pascal programs.

Prg-name in the program heading denotes the program name identifier. *File-list* denotes a list of file name identifiers and the type of operations that are permitted on them.

1.1.2 DECLARATION PART

The declaration part of a Pascal program may contain up to five sections. They are the label, constant, type, variable, and subprogram sections. An individual section is required only if an identifier is defined or declared in that particular section. Thus, if a program does not use constant identifiers, the constant section would not appear in the program. The same may be said of the other sections. However, all non-trivial programs will have at least the variable section since all identifiers, including variable identifiers, must be declared before they can be used in a Pascal program.

1.1.3 STATEMENT PART

The statement part of a Pascal program contains the executable statements that manipulate data. The statement part is actually a compound statement which always starts with a **begin** statement and concludes with an **end** statement. It has the form

begin
    statement–1;

2

statement–2;
"
"
"
statement–n;
end.

1.2 IDENTIFIERS

Identifiers denote programs, procedures, functions, constants, types, variables, and fields within records. An identifier must begin with a letter followed by any number of letters and/or digits. An identifier may not be one of the Pascal **reserved words** since the latter have special meaning in Pascal. A list of the Pascal reserved words are given in Table 1.2.1. In addition to reserved words, Pascal contains the **standard identifiers** listed in Table 1.2.2.

TABLE 1.2.1 RESERVED WORDS

and	do	forward	mod	procedure	to
array	downto	function	nil	program	type
begin	else	goto	not	record	until
case	end	if	of	repeat	var
const	file	in	or	set	while
div	for	label	packed	then	with

TABLE 1.2.2 STANDARD IDENTIFIERS

abs	eof	ln	page	rewrite	text
arctan	eoln	maxint	pred	round	true
boolean	exp	new	put	sin	trunc
char	false	odd	read	sqr	unpack
chr	get	ord	readln	sqrt	write
cos	input	output	real	succ	writeln
dispose	integer	pack	reset		

3

Standard identifiers are not reserved words and therefore may be redefined by the programmer. However, since standard identifiers have predefined meanings, it is usually not wise to do so.

Pascal is not case sensitive – that is, Pascal makes no distinction between upper case and lower case, with the exception of character and string constants. Therefore, any combination of upper and lower case may be used for user-defined identifiers, standard identifiers, and reserved words. For example, currentyear, CurrentYear, and CURRENTYEAR would denote the same identifier in a Pascal program.

1.3 STANDARD DATA TYPES

Pascal provides four standard data types. These are **integer, real, char,** and **boolean.** Integer data are the positive and negative counting numbers (e.g. 0, 322, – 1476, +91). Real data are the positive and negative numbers that either include decimal points such as 7.6 and –3.91, or are expressed as powers of 10 such as 4.6741E2 and 9.701E–03. The latter two numbers are examples of exponential notation. The "E" should be read as "times ten to the power of." Therefore, 4.6741E2 is 4.6741 times ten to the power of 2 or 467.41, and 9.701E–03 is 9.701 times ten to the power of – 3 or .009701.

Character data include all characters – letters, digits, and punctuation marks – that are found on the keyboard. Boolean data are sometimes called logical data. The two possible boolean values are **true** and **false.**

1.4 CONSTANTS, CONSTANT IDENTIFIERS, AND THE CONSTANT SECTION

Constants are quantities whose values cannot be changed

during program execution. Examples of constant values were given in Section 1.3. Often, it is useful to name constants in order to make programs more readable and easier to maintain. Constants may be named, or defined, in the constant section. The constant section begins with the reserved word **const**. If present, the constant section has the form

const
    identifier–1 = *constant–1;*
    identifier–2 = *constant–2;*
          "
          "
          "
    identifier–n = *constant–n;*

Identifier–1 through *identifier-n* are identifiers and therefore must conform to the rules for forming valid identifiers. The following is an example of a constant section:

const
          Pi = 3.141592654;
    FirstLetter = 'A';
     BaseYear = 1900;
        Cat = 'Felis';
      Okay = true;

The name Pi is given, or bound to, the real constant 3.141592654 and BaseYear is bound to the integer constant 1900. Okay is a boolean constant bound to the boolean value **true**. FirstLetter and Cat are character constants. FirstLetter is bound to the single character 'A', while Cat is bound to the string constant 'Felis'. Named constants may be used anywhere in a program where constant values may be used. For example, Pi may be used in place of 3.141592654 anywhere in the program where it is legal to use constant value 3.141592654.

5

1.5 VARIABLES AND THE VARIABLE SECTION

A variable is an identifier that the compiler associates with a memory location. The value of a variable is the value currently being stored in its memory location. The value of a variable may be changed during program execution. Variables, like constant names, are identifiers and must conform to the rules for naming identifiers.

Variables must be one of the four standard data types – integer, real, char, or boolean – or one of the types described in later chapters. The variable type determines what value is actually stored in memory. Therefore, the variable must be declared in the variable section. The variable section begins with the reserved word **var** and has the form

var
    identifier–list–1: type–1;
    identifier–list–2: type–2;
    "
    "
    "
    identifier–list–n: type–n;

    where *identifier–list* has the form
    identifier–1, identifier–2, ... identifier–m.

A typical variable section is illustrated below:

var
    Xmin, Xmax, Xcoord,
    Ymin, Ymax, Ycoord: integer;
    PlotChar: char;
    Scale: real;

1.6 PUNCTUATION

Proper punctuation is essential in Pascal programs. Each program section must be punctuated exactly as shown. Most notably, the program heading, each constant definition, each type definition (Section 3.3), and each variable declaration must be terminated with a semicolon. The statements in the statement part of the program, with the exception of the last statement, also must be terminated with a semicolon. Although not required it is permissible for the last statement in the statement section to be followed by a semicolon. A period always follows the **end** statement that concludes the program.

1.7 ARITHMETIC OPERATORS

There are six arithmetic operators in Pascal. The operators, operand types, and type of result are shown in Table 1.7.1.

TABLE 1.7.1   ARITHMETIC OPERATORS

Operator	Operation	Operands	Result
+	addition, unary plus	integer/real	integer/real
−	subtraction, unary minus	integer/real	integer/real
*	multiplication	integer/real	integer/real
/	real division	integer/real	real
div	integer division	integer	integer
mod	remainder in integer div.	integer	integer

A few examples of simple arithmetic expressions are given here. Assume that the variables I and J have been declared as integer type and X and Y have been declared as real.

1. $X * I$ 4. $X/(-Y)$
2. $I + J$ 5. $I \text{ mod } J$

7

3. $- I$ 6. I **div** J

The first expression illustrates the use of the multiplication operator. The '*' operator must always be used for multiplication. Although XI denotes multiplication in an algebraic expression, it has an entirely different meaning in Pascal. In Pascal, XI would be interpreted as a single identifier name.

Unary operators are illustrated in the third and fourth examples. Note the use of parentheses in the fourth example. The parentheses are necessary because no two operators may appear next to each other in an expression. For example, I * –J is illegal. However, I * (– J) is legal.

Operands may be integer and/or real for addition, subtraction, multiplication, and real division. For addition, subtraction, and multiplication, the result is integer if both operands are integer. The result is real if either operand is real. Real division produces real results regardless of the type of the two operands. Only integer operands are allowed for the **div** and **mod** operators. The results generated are always integer.

1.7.1 OPERATOR PRECEDENCE

Operator precedence refers to the order in which arithmetic operations are performed in an expression. Arithmetic operators are divided into two levels of precedence in Pascal – high and low. The operators '*', '/', **div**, and **mod** have high precedence, while '+' and '–' have low precedence.

When arithmetic expressions have more than one operator, high precedence operators are evaluated first, in order, from left to right. Next, low precedence operators are evaluated, in order, from left to right. The use of parentheses in arithmetic expressions can alter the order in which operators are evaluated. If an expression contains a subexpression enclosed within

8

parentheses, the subexpression is evaluated first using the rules of precedence just described. If the parentheses are nested, the innermost subexpression is evaluated first. The following algorithm may be used to evaluate arithmetic expressions by applying each rule in order beginning with Rule 1:

Rule 1. If an expression contains subexpressions (parentheses), evaluate the subexpressions first, beginning with the innermost subexpression.

Rule 2. Evaluate high precedence operators, in order from left to right.

Rule 3. Evaluate low precedence operators, in order from left to right. Return to Rule 1, if necessary.

Five examples are given to illustrate the use of these rules to evaluate an arithmetic expression. The order in which operators in an expression are evaluated is given beneath the expression. Assume that all operands have been properly declared.

```
A    −   B   *   C   +   D  div  E
     3       1       4      2

(A   −   B)  *  (C   +   D)  /   E
     1       3       2       4

(A   −   B)  *  ((C   +   D) mod E)
     1       4        2      3

A    +   B  /  (−C   *   D)  +   E
     4       3   2    1       5

A    *  (((B   −   C)  *   D)   −   E   *   F)   +   G
     5         1        2       4       3       6
```

1.8 ASSIGNMENT STATEMENT

The assignment statement is used to assign a value to a variable. It has the form

variable–identifier: = expression

Variable-identifier must be declared in the variable section of the program. *Expression* may be a constant, another variable, or a formula that must be evaluated before the value is assigned to the variable. Some examples of assignment statements are given here. Assume that all variables have been appropriately declared.

```
Percent:= 0.115;
SaveX:= X;
Sum:= Sum + Amount;
Ch:= chr(60);
C:= sqrt(sqr (A) + sqr(B));
```

In the first example, the constant, 0.115, is assigned to the variable, Percent – that is, 0.115 is stored in the memory location with which Percent has been associated.

In the second example, the value of *X* is copied to SaveX. A problem arises, however, if a value has not been assigned to X previously. When a variable is first declared, its value is undefined. Therefore, it is crucial that a value is assigned to a variable before it is used on the right-hand side of an assignment statement. Otherwise, whatever random value that happens to be stored in the variable's memory location will be used, which is probably not what the programmer intended.

The third example is interesting because it illustrates a difference between Pascal assignment statements and algebraic

10

equations. The algebraic equation, Sum = Sum + Amount, is true only if Amount equals zero. However, the Pascal assignment statement, Sum:= Sum + Amount, is interpreted differently to mean add the value currently stored in Amount's memory location to the value currently stored in Sum's memory location and store the new value in Sum's memory location.

The last two examples of assignment statements illustrate the use of function calls. The last one contains function calls nested within a function call. In this example, the function sqr(A) is evaluated first, followed by the sqr(B). The results of these calculations are summed, and the square root of this value is calculated and assigned to C.

1.9 STANDARD FUNCTIONS

Pascal provides several built-in or **standard functions**. In Pascal, a function is a subprogram that computes and returns a value. Standard functions are predefined for the programmer. They may be classified into three groups – arithmetic, ordering, and boolean. Pascal's standard functions are listed in Table 1.9.1 through Table 1.9.3 with a description of each function, type of argument, and type of value returned by each function.

TABLE 1.9.1   ARITHMETIC FUNCTIONS

Function	Description	Type of Argument	Type of Value
abs(x)	absolute value of x	integer/real	same as argument
arctan(x)	inverse tangent of x [1]	integer/real	real
cos(x)	cosine of x [2]	integer/real	real
exp(x)	e to the x power	integer/real	real
ln(x)	natural logarithm of x	integer/real	real
round(x)	x rounded	real	integer
sin(x)	sine of x [2]	integer/real	real

11

sqr(x)	x squared	integer/real	same as argument
sqrt(x)	square root of x	integer/real	real
trunc(x)	x truncated	real	integer

(1) Value returned is in radians.
(2) Value of argument x is in radians.

TABLE 1.9.2 ORDERING FUNCTIONS

Function	Description	Type of Argument	Type of Value
chr(x)	character whose ordinal value is x	integer	character
ord(x)	ordinal number of x	ordinal[3]	integer
pred(x)	predecessor of x	ordinal[3]	ordinal[3]
succ(x)	successor of x	ordinal[3]	ordinal[3]

(3) Ordinal data types are discussed in Chapter 3.

TABLE 1.9.3 BOOLEAN FUNCTIONS

Function	Description	Type of Argument	Type of Value
eof(f)	true if end-of-file, false otherwise	file[4]	boolean
eoln(f)	true if end-of-line, false otherwise	file[4]	boolean
odd(x)	true if x is odd, false otherwise	integer	boolean

(4) Text files, input, and output are presented in Chapter 4.

1.9.1 INVOKING A PASCAL FUNCTION

A Pascal function is used by making a function call. A function call usually has two parts – the function name followed by an argument contained within parentheses.

1.10 SAMPLE PROGRAM

program Circle(input, output);

```
{  Program Circle reads the radius of a circle and calcu-   }
{  lates the circumference and area of the circle and then   }
{  displays the radius, circumference, and area.             }

const
    Pi   =   3.141592654;
    Filler  = '     ';

var
    Radius,
    AreaOfCircle,
    Circumference: real;

begin
    write('Enter radius of circle >> ');
    readln(Radius);
    AreaOfCircle:= Pi * sqr(Radius);
    Circumference:= 2 * Pi * Radius;
    writeln;
    writeln('    Radius       Circumference       Area   ');
    writeln(Radius, Filler, Circumference, Filler, AreaOfCircle);
end.
```

Readln, write, and writeln are Pascal statements for input and output.[5]

_____

(5) Input/output and files are covered in Chapter 4.

13

CHAPTER 2

CONTROL STRUCTURES

2.1 CONTROL STRUCTURES

Five control structures govern the logical flow of Pascal programs. Three of these – **sequential, iteration (repetition), and selection** – are often associated with structured programming. A fourth, **procedural**, should also be added to this list, although few computer science educators or computer science textbook authors are inclined to do so.

The fifth control structure, the **goto statement**, is often considered a taboo programming structure and rightfully so. The **goto** statement decidedly is not a canon of structured programming and usually is not covered in Pascal programming courses. Nevertheless, there are a few occasions when the judicial use of the **goto** statement is warranted.

2.2 SEQUENTIAL CONTROL

Sequential control of program execution refers to the sequential execution of program statements, one after another, in the order in which they appear in the program. Sequential control of Pascal programs is governed by the compound statement. A compound statement starts with the reserved word **begin** and terminates with the reserved word **end**. Compound statements have the form:

begin
  statement–1;
  statement–2;
     "
     "
     "
  statement–n
end

2.3 BOOLEAN EXPRESSIONS

Recall that Boolean data types may be assigned one of two values, either true or false. **Boolean expressions** are assertions that have a boolean result. Selection and iteration structures, as well as other structures, incorporate boolean expressions.

A **simple boolean expression** may consist of a boolean variable, a boolean constant, a reference to a boolean-valued function, or an expression of the form

expression–1 relational-operator expression–2

where *expression–1* and *expression–2* are of the same type. **Relational-operator** is one of the operators shown in Table 2.3.1.

TABLE 2.3.1   RELATIONAL OPERATORS

<	less than
>	greater than

15

```
=      equal to
<=     less than or equal to
>=     greater than or equal to
<>     not equal to
```

Consider the assignment statement

Num1Greater:= Num1 > Num2

where Num1Greater is declared as boolean and Num1 and Num2 as real. 'Num1 > Num2' is a boolean expression. If the value of Num1 is greater than the value of Num2, then the value true is assigned to Num1Greater. Otherwise, false is assigned to Num1Greater.

Additional examples of boolean expressions are given here.

```
Side >= 10
Ch = 'Q'
X < 14.27
OddNum = odd(Num)
Rotate = Y > X + 10
```

Three boolean operators – **and, or,** and **not** – may be used to combine boolean expressions to form **compound boolean expressions**. Compound boolean expressions have the form

boolean–expression–1 boolean–operator
boolean–expression–2

where *boolean-expression* is a boolean expression of the form already described. The three boolean operators are defined in Table 2.3.2 where **p** and **q** represent boolean expressions which have one of the truth values, true or false.

16

TABLE 2.3.2   BOOLEAN OPERATORS

Boolean Operator	Boolean Expression	Definition
not	not p	negation of p
and	p and q	conjunction of p and q
or	p or q	disjunction of p or q

The negation of p is true if p is false; it is false if p is true. The conjunction of p and q is true if both p and q are true, otherwise it is false. The disjunction of p or q is false if both p and q are false, otherwise it is true. These rules are summarized by the truth table in Table 2.3.3.

TABLE 2.3.3   TRUTH TABLE ILLUSTRATING NEGATION, CONJUNCTION, AND DISJUNCTION

p	q	not p	p and q	p or q
T	T	F	T	T
T	F	F	F	T
F	T	T	F	T
F	F	T	F	F

The following precedence table illustrates the order in which operators are evaluated in boolean expressions that have combinations of relational operators, boolean operators, and/or arithmetic operators.

TABLE 2.3.4   OPERATOR PRECEDENCE

Operator	Priority
not	highest
/, *, div, mod, and	
+, −, or	
<, >, =, <=, >=, <>	lowest

17

Operators with the highest precedence in a boolean expression are evaluated first, in order, from left to right. Operators with the next highest precedence are evaluated next, and so on, until all operators have been evaluated. As with arithmetic expressions, the use of parentheses can alter the order in which operators are evaluated. Five examples of boolean expressions are shown below. The order in which operators in the expressions are evaluated is given below each expression. Assume that A, B, and C are declared as integer; X, Y, and Z as real; and P and Q as boolean.

```
X   +   10   <=  Y/Z
    2        3   1

(0  >   X)  and (X   <=  10)
    1        3        2

(X  <   Y)  or  (A   >   B)  and (B   <   C)
    1       5        2        4       3

(X  +   10  <   Y)  and (A   div  B   <   C)
    1       2        5        3        4

(A  +   B  mod  C   >   0)  and  not (p   or  q)
    2       1        3        6    5      4
```

Although logical in nature, boolean expressions can be tricky. In light of this, two cautionary notes are made here. First, the expressions that are connected by boolean operators must, themselves, be boolean. This seems obvious, but consider the following expression:

```
0 > X and X <= 10
```

In this example, **and** has the highest priority and is evaluated first. This is clearly an illegal expression since **and** cannot be applied to numeric operands. This may be more evident when parentheses are added for clarity:

0 > (X **and** X) <= 10

The addition of parentheses does not change the order of evaluation. They do, however, show more clearly that the operands for the **and** operator are numeric, not boolean, as is required. The second cautionary note pertains to boolean expressions containing real data type. It should be remembered that most real values cannot be represented exactly in computer memory. Therefore, it is possible that unexpected results may occur when using the '=' or '<>' operators to compare real values. Consider the following expression:

1.0 = X * (1.0/X)

Although this expression is always algebraically true for X <> 0, it is possible for a computer to evaluate it as false. For example, if X equals 0.1, the value calculated by a computer for the right-hand side of the expression would not be exactly 1.0. Thus, the boolean expression would be false.

2.4 SELECTION

The **selection**, or **branching, control structure** introduces decision points in programs. It is used when a program must choose between two or more possible courses of action. The computer's ability to make decisions and to execute different sequences of instructions is what enables the computer to solve a variety of problems by responding to different situations in different ways. Pascal provides two selection control structures, the **if** statement and the **case** statement.

2.4.1 THE IF STATEMENT

The **if** statement has the following forms in Pascal:

if *boolean-expression* **then**
    statement
and
if *boolean-expression* **then**
    statement–1
else
    statement–2

In the first form of the **if** statement, the *statement* portion is executed only if the boolean expression is true, otherwise it is skipped. In the second form, *statement–1* is executed if the boolean expression is true, otherwise *statement–2* is executed.

Examples of both forms of the **if** statement are given below:

```
if not EndFlag then
    Value:= Value * 10 + ord(NextDigit);

If Object = 'Circle' then
    begin
        Circumference:=  2 * Pi  * Radius;
        Area: = Pi * sqr(Radius)
    end
else {Object is a Square}
    begin
        Circumference:= 4 * Side;
        Area:= sqr(Side)
    end;
```

In the first example, the value of the variable Value is recomputed if EndFlag is false, otherwise the statement is skipped. In the second example, it is assumed that Object can

20

be a 'Circle' or a 'Square' only. However, the strict interpretation of the second example is that if Object equals 'Circle', the **if** clause is executed; if Object is not equal to 'Circle' the **else** clause is executed. Therefore, the **else** clause is executed if Object equals 'Triangle', even though this might not be what the programmer intended.

2.4.1.1 NESTED 'IF' STATEMENTS

The statement part of an **if** statement may itself be an **if** statement. In this case, the **if** statements are said to be nested. Nested **if** statements may take many forms. Several examples are given here with appropriate commentary:

EXAMPLE 1

> **if** *boolean–expression–1* **then**
> > **if** *boolean–expression–2* **then**
> > > *statement*

This form is equivalent to

> **if** *(boolean–expression–1)* **and** *(boolean-expression-2)* **then**
> > *statement*

EXAMPLE 2

> **if** *boolean–expression–1* **then**
> > **if** *boolean–expression–2* **then**
> > > *statement–1*
> > **else**
> > > *statement–2*

In this form of nested **if** statements, there are two **if** clauses and only one **else** clause. In such situations the **else** clause is always associated with the last unpaired **if** clause. In this case, the **else** is paired with the second **if** clause. Therefore, if *boolean-expression–1* is false the entire **if** block is skipped. If *boolean-expression–1* is true and *boolean-expression–2* is true, then *statement–1* is executed. If *boolean–expression–1* is true and *boolean–expression–2* is false, then *statement–2* is executed.

The question arises as to how the last example could be modified so that the single **else** clause is paired with the first **if** clause instead of the second. The following example demonstrates how this can be done.

EXAMPLE 3

if *boolean–expression–1* **then**
    begin
        if *boolean–expression–2* **then**
           statement–1
    end
else
    statement–2

If statements may be nested in such a way that a selection may be made from many alternatives, as in the next example.

EXAMPLE 4

if *boolean–expression–1* **then**
    statement–1
else
    if *boolean-expression–2* **then**
        statement–2
    else
        if *boolean-expression–3* **then**
           statement–3
        else
             ”
             ”
             ”
           statement–n

22

If there are many alternatives to choose from, Pascal provides another selection control structure to use – the **case** statement.

2.4.2 THE CASE STATEMENT

The **case** statement has the following form

```
case selector of
    case–label–list–1: statement–1;
    case–label–list–2: statement–2;
        "
        "
        "
    case–label–list–n: statement–n
end;
```

where *selector* is a variable or expression whose type is either integer, character, boolean, enumerated, or subrange[6]. The selector may not be real. The *case-label-list* is a list of values of the same type as the **case** *selector*. When the **case** statement is executed the **case** *selector* is evaluated. The statement that is associated with the *case-label-list* with a value equal to the **case** *selector*'s value is then executed. Execution then continues with the statement following the **end**.

In standard implementations of Pascal, a run-time error will occur if the value of the **case** *selector* is not found in the *case-label* list. To avoid this problem many implementations of Pascal have added an **otherwise** clause or an **else** clause to catch all **case** *selector* values not found in the *case-label* list. The following example illustrates one possible form:

```
case selector of
    case–label–list–1: statement–1;
```

[6] Enumerated and subrange types are covered in Chapter 3.

case–label–list–2: statement–2;
```
"
"
"
```
case–label–list–n: statement–n
otherwise {or **else**}
   statement
end;

Note that the **case** statement does not have a **begin**, but it is always terminated with an **end**.

An example of a standard implementation of the **case** statement is shown below:

```
case ErrorCode of
    1: writeln('**** File not found ****');
    2: writeln('**** File already exists ****');
    3: writeln('**** Illegal file type ****');
    4: writeln('**** Illegal file name ****');
    5: writeln('**** Insufficient disk space ****');
    6: writeln('**** Invalid directory ****');
    7: writeln('**** Disk not formatted ****');
    8: writeln('**** Error writing to device ****');
 9, 19: writeln('**** Invalid parameter ****');
   10: writeln('**** Check printer ****');
end;
```

2.5   ITERATION

Iteration – or **repetition** – **control structures** make it possible to repeat the execution of one or more statements. Iteration control structures are often called **loops** for this reason. Pascal provides three iteration control structures – the **for** loop, the **while** loop, and the **repeat** loop.

24

2.5.1   THE FOR STATEMENT

The **for** statement has two forms:

and
> for *control–variable:= initial–value* **to** *final–value* **do**
>   *statement*

> for *control–variable:= initial–value* **downto** *final–value* **do**
>   *statement*

where *control–variable* is of type integer, character, boolean, enumerated, or subrange[7]. *Initial-value* and *final-value* may be any legal Pascal expression, but they must be of the same type as the *control–variable*. Also note that, as always, *statement* may be either a simple Pascal statement or a compound statement.

When the **for** statement in the **to** form is executed, the *control-varlable* is assigned the initial value and the **body** of the **for** statement is executed provided that the initial value is not larger than the final value. The *control–variable* is incremented by one and if it is still less than or equal to the final value, the body of the **for** statement is executed again. This process continues until the *control-variable* is greater than the final value. In the **downto** form of the **for** statement, the *control-variable* is decremented until its value is less than the final value. The *control-variable*, the *initial-value*, and the *final-value* may not be altered by the body of the **for** loop.

The **for** statement should be used whenever the loop can be controlled by a simple counter that can be incremented or decremented by one. The **for** statement cannot be used if the loop is event driven. A loop is event driven if the number of times that the loop executes is determined by an event – one or more

---

(7) Enumerated and subrange types are covered in Chapter 3.

statements – in the body of the loop.

Two examples of the **for** statement are shown below:

```
for Ch:= 'A' to 'Z' do
   writeln(Ch, Space, ord(Ch));

readln(Num2);
for := 1 to Num2 do
   begin
      readln(Num2);
      if odd(Num2) then
         Sum:= Sum + 1
      else
         Sum:= Sum + Num2 div 2
   end
writeln(sum);
```

2.5.2   THE WHILE STATEMENT

The **while** statement has the form

while *boolean-expression* **do**
statement

The **while** statement is sometimes called a **pretest loop** since the boolean expression is evaluated before the body of the loop is executed. If the expression is false, the body of the loop is not executed at all. If the boolean expression is true, the body of the loop is executed. The boolean expression is re-evaluated and if true the body of the loop is executed again. This process is repeated until the boolean expression becomes false.

The **while** statement is event-driven since the body of the loop must affect the boolean expression in such a way that the boolean expression eventually becomes false. If it doesn't, the program enters an infinite loop – the **while** statement is executed *ad infinitum.*

The **while** statement should be used if the loop is event-controlled and nothing is known about the loop's first execution – that is the programmer may not know in advance whether the body of the **while** statement will be executed at least once.

An example of the **while** statement is shown below:

```
CharCount:= 0;
while not eof(infile) do
    begin
            read(infile,Ch);
            if ch <> BlankSpace then
                CharCount:= succ(CharCount)
    end;
```

2.5.3 THE REPEAT STATEMENT

The **repeat** statement is a **post-test loop**. The boolean expression controlling its execution is tested after the statements in the body of the loop have been executed. The **repeat** statement has the form

```
repeat
    statement–1;
    statement–2;
        "
        "
        "
    statement–n
until boolean–expression
```

When the **repeat** statement is executed, *statement–1* through *statement–n* are executed. Next the boolean expression is evalu-

27

ated. If it is false the body of the **repeat** statement is executed again. Then the boolean expression is re-evaluated. This process continues until the boolean expression is true.

Like the **while** statement, the **repeat** statement is event-driven. That is, the statements in the body of the **repeat** must affect the evaluation of the boolean expression in such a way that the latter eventually becomes true. Otherwise, the program becomes locked in an infinite loop. Unlike the **while** statement, whose body may never be executed, the body of the **repeat** statement is always executed at least once. Therefore, the **repeat** statement may be selected only if the loop is event-driven and only if the loop will be executed at least once no matter what conditions exist when the loop is first encountered.

Both the **while** statement and the **repeat** statement are appropriate in many circumstances in which the loop will be executed at least once. In such situations, choose the one that better reflects the semantics of the problem associated with the boolean expression. If the problem is stated in terms of when to keep looping, select the **while** statement. If the problem is stated in terms of when to stop looping, select the **repeat** statement.

An example of the **repeat** statement follows:

```
Sum:= 0;
Num:= 0;
repeat
    Sum:= Sum + Num;
    read(Num)
until Num < 0;
writeln(Sum);
```

2.6 PROCEDURAL CONTROL STRUCTURES

It is not uncommon to find identical segments of code or

near identical segments of code repeated two or more times in large programs. In Pascal, it is possible to replace redundant segments of code with single statements which invoke a **procedure** or a **function** containing the displaced code.[8] Clearly, one of the advantages of this feature is that redundant code is removed from a program. Another advantage is that the program is more readable.

2.7 LABELS, THE LABEL SECTION, AND THE GOTO STATEMENT

Ninety-nine programs out of 100 should be written with only the four control structures already presented – sequential, selection, iteration, and procedural. These control structures lend themselves to modular, well-structured, and easily readable and maintainable programs.

There are rare situations in which the use of only these four control structures is awkward or inefficient. For example, an error or other exceptional situation arises during a process that requires the suspension of the process. In such situations, the **goto** statement may be used.

The **goto** statement is used to transfer program control to a statement that is prefixed by a **label**. The **label** must be declared in the label declaration section immediately following the program heading. The label section has the following form:

label
  label–1, label–2, ... label–n;

Each *label* is a positive integer from one to four digits. A label may be used to label only one statement. The label appears as a

---

(8) Procedures and functions are covered in Chapter 5.

prefix to a statement as follows:

label: statement

Program control can be transferred to the labeled statement by using a **goto** statement:

goto *label*

The general rule for using **goto**s is to use them only when absolutely necessary. Use only sequential, selection, iteration, and procedural control structures whenever it is reasonably possible. Careless use of **goto**s may lead to unreadable and difficult to maintain programs.

An example of **label** declarations and the use of **goto** statements is illustrated below:

```
label 100;
    "
    "
    "
begin
    "
    "
    "
    if token <> 'Program' then
        begin
            writeln('*** Error: "Program" expected ***');
            goto 100
        end
    "
    "
    "
100: end;
```

2.8   SAMPLE PROGRAM

The following program illustrates some of the structures that were presented in this Chapter.

```
program Calcpower(input,output);

{  Program Calcpower finds X raised to the Nth Power. The   }
{  algorithm used in the program works only for values of X  }
{  greater than zero. Therefore, the repeat loop checks the  }
{  value of X to ensure that it is greater than zero. Note that  }
{  the writeln formats the values of X, N and Power. In the  }
{  case of X and Power which are real numbers, the output  }
{  will be written in decimal form with a total of six positions  }
{  (including the decimal) with two decimal places. The  }
{  value of N will be formatted as a two digit integer.  }

var
        X,
        Power: real;
        I,
        N:  integer;
begin
        repeat
            write('Enter X and N: ');
            read(X,N);
            writeln
        until X > 0;
        Power:= 1;
        for I:= 1 to abs(N) do
            Power:= Power * X;
        if N < 0 then
        Power:= 1/Power;
        writeln(X:6:2,'^',N:2,' = ', Power:6:2);
end.
```

CHAPTER 3

ORDINAL DATA TYPES

3.1 DATA TYPES

Pascal supports many data types, both predefined and user-defined, as Figure 3.1 illustrates.

FIGURE 3.1   DATA TYPES SUPPORTED BY PASCAL

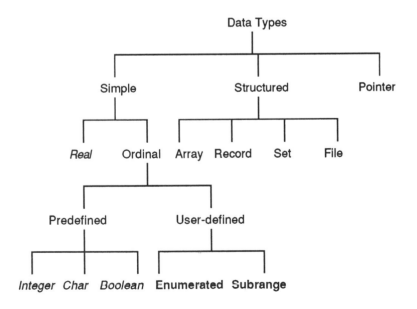

The four standard data types supported by Pascal were introduced in Chapter 1. These include real, integer, char, and boolean. Sometimes they are referred to as **simple** predefined data types. Simple data types are atomic in nature, that is, they cannot be subdivided.

The concept of **ordinal** data types is introduced in the next section. This is followed by a discussion of the two user-defined ordinal types supported by Pascal, namely **enumerated** and **subrange**.

3.2   STANDARD ORDINAL DATA TYPES

An ordinal data type is an ordered set in which every element, except the first element, has an immediate predecessor, and every element, except the last element, has an immediate successor. Integer, char, and boolean types are standard ordinal data types. Real type is not ordinal because a real value has no unique predecessor or successor. By adding additional digits of precision, the predecessor and successor of real values change. For example, is 8.061, 8.0601, 8.06001, or 8.060001 the immediate successor of 8.06? The answer is none of them. Another digit can be added to obtain a more immediate successor – or predecessor.

3.3   TYPE SECTION

The general structure of a Pascal program was introduced in Chapter 1. One of the sections that may be present in the declaration part of a program is the **type** section. If present, the type section has the form

type
    identifier–1 = type 1;
    identifier–2 = type 2;

"

"

"

identifier–3 = type–n;

Identifier–1 through *identifier–n* are identifiers which conform to the rules for forming valid identifiers. The following example illustrates the use of the **type** section.

```
type
    Status    =  boolean;
    Register  =  integer;

var
    Carry, Zero, Negative: Status;
    AX, BX, CX: Register;
```

In this example, the variables Carry, Zero, and Negative are declared as type Status where Status is type boolean. Likewise, AX, BX, and CX are declared as type Register where the latter is type integer.

3.4 ENUMERATED DATA TYPES

Enumerated data types comprise one of the two classes of user-defined ordinal data types supported by Pascal. Enumerated data types have the form

identifier = (const–ident–1, const–ident–2, ... const-ident-n);

An example illustrating the use of enumerated data types is shown below:

```
type
    ExoticColors = (Fuchsia, Magenta, Indigo, Teal, Ecru);
    PrimaryColor = (Red, Blue, Yellow);
```

34

var
    Paint: ExoticColor
    Trim: PrimaryColor;

There are a few basic rules regarding the usage of enumerated data types. They are summarized in Table 3.4.1.

TABLE 3.4.1   RULES GOVERNING USAGE OF ENUMERATED DATA TYPES

Rule 1. A constant identifier cannot appear in more than one enumerated type declaration.

Rule 2. Since enumerated data types are ordinal – an ordered set – relational operators (<, >, =, <=, >=, <>) may be used to compare enumerated type values. This means that enumerated type values may be used in boolean expressions of control structures such as **while, for,** and **repeat** loops, and **if...then...else** statements.

Rule 3. Pred, succ, and ord functions are also applicable with enumerated type values for the reason given in Rule 2.

Rule 4. Values of enumerated data types cannot be read from or written to text files.

The examples that follow demonstrate the implementation of these rules using the declarations given earlier on colors.

EXAMPLE 1

    for Paint:= Fuchsia **to** Ecru **do**
        begin

```
"

"

"
```
end;

EXAMPLE 2

```
Paint:= pred(Indigo);
Paint:= succ(Ecru);
```

The pred(Indigo) is Magenta. Paint becomes undefined in the second statement since Ecru is the last element in the set and has no successor. This statement will generate a run-time error when it is executed.

EXAMPLE 3.

```
ColorNumber:= ord(Teal);
```

The ord(Teal) is 3. Ord returns the value of the position of the element in the enumerated type. Position numbering begins with zero for the first element.

EXAMPLE 4

```
case Paint of
   Fuchsia:  writeln('Fuchsia');
   Magenta:  writeln('Magenta');
    Indigo:  writeln('Indigo');
      Teal:  writeln('Teal');
      Ecru:  writeln('Ecru');
end;
```

Values of enumerated types cannot be read from or written to text files. This also applies to standard input/output files. This example illustrates one method for outputting text equivalents of enumerated types.

36

3.5 SUBRANGE DATA TYPES

Ordinal types discussed thus far represent entire ranges of values. It is also possible to define a **subrange type** to be a subrange of an existing ordinal type. The existing ordinal type is known as the base type, which can be one of the standard ordinal types or an enumerated type.

The form of the subrange type is given below:

identifier = lower–bound–value ... upper–bound–value;

where *lower–bound–value* and *higher–bound–value* are values of some ordinal base type and *lower–bound–value* is lower than or equal to *upper–bound–value*. Rules that govern the use of ordinal types apply to a subrange of the ordinal type.

A value of one data type can be assigned to a variable of another data type only if the two data types are compatible. Two data types are compatible if they have the same definition, if they have the same type identifier, if one is a subrange of the other, or if both are subranges of the same base type. An error is generated otherwise.

The major advantage of using subrange types is automatic range checking. By specifying exactly the range of legal values that a variable may take on, the compiler will check to ensure that only values within the specified subrange are assigned to the variable.

Here are two examples of subrange data type definitions followed by the corresponding variable declarations:

```
type
      DayOfWeek = (Monday, Tuesday, Wednesday,
```

```
                Thursday, Friday, Saturday, Sunday);
    WeekDay = Monday ... Friday;
    WeekEnd = Saturday ... Sunday;

var
    WorkDay:    WeekDay;
    PlayDay:    WeekEnd;
```

The subrange type definition and the variable declaration may be combined in one statement.

```
type
    DayOfWeek = (Monday, Tuesday, Wednesday,
                 Thursday, Friday, Saturday, Sunday);

var
    WorkDay:    Monday ... Friday;
    PlayDay:    Saturday ... Sunday;
```

These two examples are actually identical. However, the first example provides more flexibility for program development since it allows Workday and Playday to be passed as parameters to procedures and functions. If Workday and Playday are declared as they are in the second example, they cannot be passed as parameters to procedures and functions. Procedures and functions are presented in Chapter 5.

3.6 SAMPLE PROGRAM

program EstimateMood(input,output);

```
{   The program reads your mood ratings as rated by other   }
{   individuals from the keyboard until a Ctrl-Z is entered.  }
{   The Ctrl-Z is interpreted as the end-of-file (eof) in the  }
{   first while loop. After the AverageRating of YourRating is  }
```

{   calculated, YourMood is assigned the value of Melan-   }
{   choly, which is lowest value of **type** Mood. YourMood is }
{   incremented as long as its ord value is not equal to the   }
{   AverageRating minus one. The case statement outputs   }
{   a message based upon the value of YourMood.   }

```
type
        Mood  = (Melancholy, Gloomy, Sullen, Capricious,
                   Pensive, Sober, Humorous, Jubilant,
                   Elated, Ecstatic);

        Rating = 1 ... 10;

var
        YourMood: Mood;
        YourRating, AverageRating: Rating;
        SumOfRatings, NumberOfRaters: integer;

begin
        SumOfRatings:= 0;
        NumberOfRaters:= 0;
        while not eof do
           begin
                readln(YourRating);
                SumOfRatings:= SumOfRatings + YourRating;
                NumberOfRaters:= succ(NumberOfRaters);
           end;
        writeln;
        AverageRating:= round(SumOfRatings /
                                        NumberOfRaters);
        YourMood:= Melancholy;
        while ord(YourMood) <> AverageRating − 1 do
           YourMood:= succ(YourMood);
        case YourMood of
           Melancholy: writeln
                   ('Make an appointment with your analyst.');
```

```
        Gloomy: writeln('Go back to bed.');
        Sullen: writeln('Cheer up. Things could be worse.');
        Capricious: writeln('Don''t be so fickle.');
        Pensive: writeln('Enroll in a college course.');
        Sober: writeln('Today you should be mischievous.');
        Humorous: writeln
              ('Get serious. It may mean a promotion.');
        Jubilant: writeln
              ('Go on a shopping spree. You  deserve it.');
        Elated: writeln('Ask Your boss for a raise.');
        Ecstatic: writeln('Spread the cheer!');
      end;
      writeln('Your rating is ',AverageRating);
end.
```

CHAPTER 4

FILES AND INPUT/OUTPUT OPERATIONS

4.1 FILES

The advantage of writing computer programs is that they can be used with different sets of data. To achieve this flexibility, data must be kept separate from the program. When data values have been stored in variables, a program can manipulate the data values producing sought-after results. New values can be stored in the variables without changing the program and the program can be executed again. To accomplish this flexibility, data are stored separately from the program in a file. A **file** is a collection of data items, usually stored in secondary memory, that is, input to or output by a program.

4.1.1 STANDARD SYSTEM FILES – INPUT/OUTPUT FILES

Pascal provides two standard system files, one called **input** and one called **output**. Generally, these files are associated with the terminal device and are used for interactive processing. The input and output files do not have to be opened by the program. They are opened automatically for the programmer.

Pascal often has difficulties with interactive processing. Consider, for example, the following program segment:

```
"

"

"

while not eof do
    begin
        write('Enter value: ');
        readln(num);
    end;
"

"

"
```

A potential problem exists with the eof in the **while** statement. Eof returns true if the end of the input file has been reached. Otherwise, it returns false. In this case, however, the program may be unable to determine the status of the input file if the boolean check is made before any read operations have been performed on the file. Generally, the program will appear to hang until some value is entered and then the prompt will appear. To overcome this problem, many implementations of Pascal provide a special interface or set of procedures to handle interactive processing.

4.1.2   TEXT FILES

Like the standard system file input, text files consist of a sequence of characters. Each line of text contains data items separated by spaces and terminated with an end-of-line mark. The file is terminated with an end-of-file mark. Pascal provides two standard functions that detect these marks, namely, **eoln** and **eof**.

Text files are accessed through file variables which are declared as **type text**. The following example demonstrates the declaration of a file variable:

var
    RatingInfo: text;

In addition, the file name must appear in the program heading such as

program EstimateMood(output, RatingInfo);

4.2 INPUT OPERATIONS ON TEXT FILES

Before a text file can be read it must be opened. The **reset statement** is used to open a text file for input. It has the form:

reset(*file–variable*)

Therefore, to open the file RatingInfo for input the statement becomes

reset(RatingInfo);

Many implementations of Pascal use a modified form of this method to open a file for input that associates the logical file name used in the program with the actual physical file name that is used by the computer. One method used is to modify the reset statement as follows

reset(*file–variable, file–name*)

where *file–variable* is the program variable that is associated with the actual *file–name* used by the computer.

Another common method is to use a separate statement called **assign** that performs the binding between the logical file name used by the program and the actual physical file name. In such implementations the standard form of the reset statement is used to open the file.

Two Pascal statements may be used to input information once a text file is opened. However, before covering these statements, the reader must first understand the concept of a file marker. A file marker may be thought of as a pointer that points to the next data item in the file that is available for processing. When a file is opened with the reset statement the file marker is set to the beginning of the file. As the file is processed, the file marker is automatically advanced as data items are read from the file.

Two statements – the **read statement** and the **readln statement** – are used to input information from a text file into a program. The read statement has the form

read(*file–variable, parameter–1, parameter–2, ... parameter–n*)

where *file-variable* refers to the file to be read. The file's data are read into the program variables specified in the parameter list *parameter–1* through *parameter–n*. The reason that the items are referred to as parameters is that the read and readln statements, as well as the write and writeln statements, are actually standard Pascal procedures. An example of a read statement is shown below:

read(StudentFile, Grade1, Grade2, Grade3, Average);

where StudentFile is the *file–variable*, and Grade1, Grade2, Grade3, and Average make up the parameter list.

Data values that are read from the file must be of the same type as the variables into which the data values are placed. For example, assume that Grade1, Grade2, and Grade3 have been declared as type integer and Average has been declared as type real. Then the three data values that are read from the file StudentFile into the three variables Grade1, Grade2, and Grade3 must be of type integer. Likewise, the data value read from the file into the variable Average must be of type real. Otherwise, an error is generated.

The single read statement above could have been written as two, three, or four separate statements. For example, the read statement shown previously is equivalent to the following:

```
read(StudentFile, Grade1, Grade2, Grade3);
read(StudentFile, Average);
```

The readln statement has the same form as the read statement:

readln(*file–variable, parameter–1, parameter–2, ... parameter–n)*

The difference between the read statement and the readln statement is that the readln statement advances the file marker to the beginning of the next line in the file after the data have been read into the program. The read statement does not advance the file marker to the next line. This means that the readln statement may be used to skip remaining data on a line. Another difference between the two statements is that the readln statement may be used without a parameter list while the read statement may not.

4.2.1   EOF AND EOLN FUNCTIONS

Eof is a standard boolean function that may be used to detect the end of a file. It is often necessary to make this check because attempting to read beyond the end-of-file mark will generate an error. A call to eof has the form:

eof(*file–variable*)

The standard file input is assumed if the *file-variable* and parentheses are omitted. Eof returns the value true if the file marker is positioned at the end-of-file mark. Otherwise, it returns the value false.

Likewise, the function **eoln** may be used to detect the end-of-line mark. Eoln returns true if the file marker is positioned at an end-of-line mark. Otherwise, it returns the value false. A call to eoln has the form

eoln(*file–variable*)

If the *file–variable* and parentheses are omitted, the standard system file input is assumed.

Most implementations of Pascal provide a **close** procedure to close a text file when the processing of the file has been completed. When an implementation of Pascal provides a close procedure, it is always wise to use it to close a text file when processing of the file has been completed. This is particularly true if the text file has been used for output. Failure to close a file that has been written to could result in lost data.

4.3 OUTPUT OPERATIONS ON TEXT FILES

Just as with input, a text file must be opened before information can be written to it. The **rewrite statement** is used to open a text file for output. It has the form

rewrite(*file–variable*)

The implementation dependent variations for opening input text files also apply to opening output text files. Furthermore, as before, the *file–variable* must be declared as type text and must appear in the program heading.

When a file is opened with the rewrite statement, the file marker is set to the beginning of the file. If the file already exists, this action will effectively erase all data in the file. Therefore, programmers always want to be careful that they do not accidentally open an input file with the rewrite statement. Otherwise, they will have to restore their input file.

Two statements may be used to output data to a file once the file has been opened with the rewrite statement. They are **write** and **writeln**. In their simplest form they have the form

write(*file–variable, parameter–1, parameter–2, ... parameter-n*)

and

writeln(*file–variable, parameter–1, parameter–2, ... paremeter-n*)

The standard system file output is assumed if the *file–variable* is omitted. The difference between the write and writeln statements is that the latter will advance the file marker to a new line after output is completed, while the former will not. Therefore, several consecutive write statements may be used to write data to the same line in the file.

Both the write and writeln statements may be used to output literals – constant values – as well as a combination of literals and parameter values. Two examples are shown below:

EXAMPLE 1

writeln('Your monthly payment will be ', MonthlyPayment);

EXAMPLE 2

```
write(OutFile,'Score 1 = ', Score1);
write(OutFile,'   Score 2 = ',  Score2);
writeln(OutFile);
```

In example one, output is directed to the standard system file output. In example two, two write statements are used to output information to one line of the file OutFile. The writeln is used to advance the file marker to a new line in the file.

In both examples, the output might appear somewhat awkward. There probably will be several blank spaces between the literal that is being output and the variable value that follows the literal. Or in the case of example 1, MonthlyPayment may be output in exponential form (scientific notation). This can be corrected in most implementations of Pascal by formatting the variable value that is output. Assuming that MonthlyPayment is type real and Score1 and Score2 are type integer, the output can be modified as follows:

EXAMPLE 3

```
writeln('Your monthly payment will be ', MonthlyPayment:7:2);
```

EXAMPLE 4

```
write(OutFile,'Score 1 = ', Score1:3);
write(OutFile,'   Score 2 = ',  Score2:3);
writeln(OutFile);
```

The output for Example 3 will look something like

Your monthly payment will be 1345.32

For example 4, the output will look like the following:

Score 1 = 245   Score 2 = 266

4.4 OTHER TYPES OF FILES

Elements in a text file are always of type **char**. It is possible for the elements of a file to be of any predefined or user-defined data type except for another file type. This includes files of enumerated types, files of type integer, files of record types, and more. Examples of several file declarations are shown below:

```
type
    Colors = (Red, Blue, Yellow, Orange, Purple, Green);
    Rating = 1..10;
    FileOfColors = file of Colors;
    FileOfNumbers = file of integer;
    FileOfRating = file of Rating;

var
    ColorFile: FileOfColors;
    NumFile: FileOfNumbers;
    RatingFile: FileOfRating;
    Color: Colors;
    CurrentRating: Rating;
```

The statements reset, rewrite, read, and write may be used on nontext files. So may the functions eof and eoln. Assume the type definitions and variable declarations given above. The following program segment illustrates some of these principles.

```
            "
            "
            "
    rewrite(ColorFile);
    Color:= Red;
    write(ColorFile,Color);
    Color:= Blue;
```

```
write(ColorFile,Color);
     "
     "
     "
reset(RatingFile);
while not eof(RatingFile) do
   begin
      read(RatingFile, CurrentRating);
      writeln(CurrentRating);
   end;
     "
     "
     "
close(ColorFile);
close(RatingFile);
     "
     "
     "
```

Note that in this implementation, a close statement is used to close both files.

Output to a file actually takes place in two steps. In the first step, the value stored in the variable is transferred to a special variable called a file buffer variable. The file buffer variable is created automatically when a file is opened. In the example above the statement

```
rewrite(ColorFile);
```

creates the file buffer variable which is denoted by ColorFile^.

Once data have been transferred to the file buffer variable the data are written to the file by a **put procedure**. Therefore,

```
write(ColorFile, Color);
```

is equivalent to

```
ColorFile^:= Color;
put(ColorFile);
```

Input from a file is analogous to output to a file. When a file is opened with the reset statement two actions are carried out. First, the file buffer variable is created, and second, the first set of data in the file is copied from the file into the file buffer variable. Third, the data are transferred from the file buffer variable to the program variable. Therefore,

```
read(RatingFile, CurrentRating);
```

is equivalent to

```
CurrentRating:= RatingFile^;
get(RatingFile);
```

There are some advantages to using the get statement instead of the read statement. Many applications required lookahead capability. The use of the file buffer variable and the get statement not only makes this possible but easy to do.

Before closing this section, it is important to note that some implementations of Pascal do not support the file buffer variable, the put statement, and the get statement. In such cases, the programmer must use the read and write statements for input from and output to a nontext file.

4.5   SAMPLE PROGRAM

program EstimateMood(RatingFile, Output);

{   This program is a modified version of the program given   }

51

```
{   in Section 3.4. It reads ratings from a file of type Rating.   }
{   Note that this implementation uses a close statement to        }
{   close the file when processing is done.                        }

type
        Mood = (Melancholy, Gloomy, Sullen, Capricious,
                Pensive, Sober, Humorous, Jubilant,
                Elated, Ecstatic);
        Rating = 1 ... 10;
        FileOfRating = file of Rating;

var
        YourMood: Mood;
        YourRating, AverageRating: Rating;
        SumOfRatings, NumberOfRaters: integer;
        RatingFile: FileOfRating;

begin
        reset(RatingFile);
        SumOfRatings:= 0;
        NumberOfRaters:= 0;
        while not eof (RatingFile) do
            begin
                read(RatingFile, YourRating);
                SumOfRatings:= SumOfRatings + YourRating;
                NumberOfRaters:= succ(NumberOfRaters);
            end;
        writeln;
        AverageRating:= round(SumOfRatings /
                                    NumberOfRaters);
        YourMood:= Melancholy;
        while ord(YourMood) <> AverageRating – 1 do
            YourMood:= succ(YourMood);
        case YourMood of
            Melancholy: writeln
```

```
                   ('Make an appointment with your analyst.');
          Gloomy: writeln('Go back to bed.');
          Sullen: writeln('Cheer up. Things could be worse.');
          Capricious: writeln('Don''t be so fickle.');
          Pensive: writeln
                   ('Enroll in a college course on Greek Mythology.');
          Sober: writeln('Today you should be mischievous.');
          Humorous: writeln
                   ('Be serious today. It may mean a promotion.');
          Jubilant: writeln
                   ('Go on a shopping spree. You  deserve it.');
          Elated: writeln('Ask Your boss for a raise.');
          Ecstatic: writeln('Spread the cheer!');
        end;
        writeln('Your rating is ',AverageRating);
        close(RatingFile);
end.
```

CHAPTER 5

PROCEDURES AND FUNCTIONS

5.1 PROCEDURES

The programs that were presented in previous chapters are monolithic in nature. Most problems requiring the application of a computer, however, are too complex to be solved with such a brute force approach. Therefore, a **top-down** approach that employs a **divide-and-conquer** strategy is used to solve complex problems. This strategy calls for the programmer to divide the problem repeatedly into simpler subproblems until each subproblem can be solved easily. Separate algorithms, which are developed for each subproblem, are translated into subprograms or modules. Finally, these modules are combined into a single program in such a way that the program solves the original problem. Pascal supports top-down strategy and modular programming by providing subprogram structures known as procedures and functions.

A **procedure** is a subprogram that usually performs a single task. Information is passed between a procedure and the calling module via parameters. A Pascal **procedure definition** is nearly identical to a program. However, a **procedure heading** contains an optional **parameter list**, and the procedure definition is terminated with a semicolon instead of a period. A procedure definition is placed in the subprogram section immediately following the variable (**var**) section. The reader is referred to Chapter 1 for a review of program structure and organization.

5.1.1   PROCEDURE HEADING

The procedure heading has the form:

procedure *identifier;*

or

procedure *identifier(formal–parameter–list)*;

where *formal–parameter–list* has the form

parameter–group–1; parameter–group–2; ...
parameter–group–n

A *parameter–group* has the form

identifier–1, identifier–2, ... identifier–m: identifier–type

or

var *identifier–1, identifier–2, ... identifier–m: identifier–type*

Several examples of procedure headings are given below in order to illustrate the varied possibilities:

procedure DisplayMenu;

procedure WriteRecord(OutRecord: RecordType);

```
procedure ReadRecord(var InFile: text;
                     var InRecord: RecordType);

procedure Rotate(var X, Y, Z: integer);

procedure NextGeneration(var Cell, Copy: Automaton;
                         Rule: Rules);

procedure PushStack(var S: Stack; I: Item);
```

The first procedure heading does not have the optional *formal-parameter–list*. The next five examples do. Some of the *parameter-groups* in these examples begin with the reserved word **var** while others do not. The presence or absence of **var** determines the manner in which information is passed to procedures. Its implications on parameter passing will be explained in a moment. The fourth and fifth examples show how more than one formal parameter may be declared with the same type.

Let's consider an example in more detail. In Chapter 3 two methods of declaring WorkDay were presented which use the following type definitions:

```
type
    DayOfWeek = (Monday, Tuesday, Wednesday,
                 Thursday, Friday, Saturday, Sunday);
    WeekDay   = Monday . . Friday;
```

WorkDay may be declared as a formal parameter in a procedure heading using the following method:

```
procedure GetDailySchedule(var Infile: Calendar;
                           var Workday: Weekday);
```

However, Workday could not be declared as a formal parameter using the following method:

```
procedure GetDailySchedule(var Infile: Calendar;
                            var Workday: Monday .. Friday);
```

5.1.2 PROCEDURE INVOCATION

A procedure may be invoked or called by a **procedure reference statement** containing the procedure name followed by an optional list of **actual parameters**. It has the form

```
identifier (actual-parameter-list)
```

The `actual-parameter-list` is a list of actual parameters that are associated with the formal parameters in the procedure heading. The number of actual parameters must be the same as the number of parameters in the formal parameter list of the procedure heading. Likewise, each actual parameter must have the same type as the formal parameter in the same position.

Consider the **procedure** Swap given below:

```
procedure Swap(var X, Y: integer);

var
    Temp: integer;

begin
    Temp:= X;
        X:= Y;
        Y:= Temp;
end;
```

Swap may be invoked by the following procedure reference statement:

```
Swap(A, B);
```

where A and B are declared as type integer. In this example, the actual parameter A is associated with the formal parameter X, and B is associated with Y.

5.1.3 PARAMETER TYPES

There are two methods of passing parameters in Pascal – **pass–by–reference** and **pass–by–value**. When parameters are passed by reference, the formal parameters in a parameter group of the procedure heading are preceded by the reserved word **var** and therefore are called **variable parameters**. Parameters are passed by value when formal parameters in a parameter group are not preceded with the reserved word **var**. They are called **value parameters**.

When parameters are passed by reference, information may be transferred into and out of a procedure via the variable parameters. This is because the **location** (address in memory) of the actual parameters are passed to the formal parameters and not their values. There is only one copy of information, which is used by both the calling routine and the procedure. When the procedure is called, the formal parameters and actual parameters become synonyms for the same locations in memory. Any change made to the value of a formal parameter will be found in the actual parameter when control is returned to the calling routine.

Consider the **procedure** Swap from above. If Swap is called with A = 10 and B = 20, X becomes synonymous with A and Y with B. The values of X and Y are exchanged by Swap so that when control is returned to the calling routine, A will have the value 20 and B will have the value 10.

When parameters are passed by value, information may be transferred into a procedure but not out of the procedure. In this case, another copy of the information is made and passed to the

58

procedure. Consider the following procedure:

```
procedure CalculateAbsoluteDifference(var Diff:
                          NonNegInt; X, Y: NonNegInt);

begin
    If X > Y then
        Swap(X,Y);
    Diff:= Y − X;
end;
```

Suppose that CalculateAbsoluteDifference is invoked with the following procedure reference statement:

```
CalculateAbsoluteDifference(Difference,A,B);
```

with $A = 20$ and $B = 10$. The starting value of Difference is not of any consequence in this case. The value of A is copied and passed to X and the value of B is copied and passed to Y. Since X is greater than Y, the values of X and Y will be exchanged. However, since the values of A and B were passed to the procedure and not their addresses, A will still have the value 20 and B will still have the value 10 when control is returned to the calling routine.

5.1.4   NESTED SUBPROGRAM DEFINITIONS

Procedures may be defined within procedures. Swap, for example, could be defined within CalculateAbsoluteDifference:

```
procedure CalculateAbsoluteDifference(var Diff:
                          NonNegInt; X, Y: NonNegInt);

    procedure Swap(var X, Y: integer);

    var Temp: integer;
```

```
begin {procedure Swap}
    Temp:=  X;
      X:=  Y;
      Y:=  Temp;
end;   {procedure Swap}


begin {procedure  CalculateAbsoluteDifference}
    If X > Y then
        Swap(X,Y);
    Diff:= Y − X;
end;   {procedure  CalculateAbsoluteDifference}
```

5.1.5   FORWARD DECLARATION OF SUBPROGRAMS

A basic Pascal maxim regarding subprograms is that they must be declared before they are invoked. Occasionally, this maxim creates a dilemma for the programmer. Consider, for example, two procedures each calling the other. Which procedure should the programmer declare first? Regardless of the choice, one of the two procedures will be invoked before it has been declared.

This dilemma is actually created by the compiler. The compiler, which makes two passes through the source code, enters all constant, variable, and subprogram identifiers into a symbol table on its first pass. If the compiler encounters an identifier which has not been declared, such as a procedure identifier in a procedure reference statement, it will generate an error message. How then can the programmer's dilemma be overcome?

Pascal provides the **forward** declaration which tells the compiler that a subprogram identifier is valid. The **forward** declaration has the form

procedure *identifier(formal–parameter–list);* **forward;**

The procedure must be declared later within the subprogram declaration section. A partially coded example follows:

procedure DeclaredLater(*parameter list*); **forward**

procedure DeclaredHere(*parameter list*);

local declarations

begin
    "
    "
    "
    DeclaredLater(*argument list*);
    "
    "
    "
end;

procedure DeclaredLater; {Omit parameter list}

local declarations

begin
    "
    "
    "
    DeclaredHere(*argument list*);
    "
    "
    "
end;

Although the formal parameter list is omitted when the **procedure** DeclaredLater is actually declared, it is wise to include a comment statement listing them for documentation purposes.

5.2 FUNCTIONS

A **function** is a subprogram that is called from within an expression, and ordinarily computes and returns a single value to the calling routine via the function name. Pascal provides several predefined functions which were presented in section 1.8. Pascal also provides the means for programmers to define their own functions.

Like procedures, user-defined functions are declared in the subprogram section. The declaration and statement parts of a function declaration also have the same form as for procedures. The function heading is different, however, and has the following form:

function *identifier: identifier–type;*

or

function *identifier(formal–parameter–list): identifier–type;*

Another feature of functions is that at least one of the statements in the statement part must assign a value to the identifier that names the function. Two examples of a function definition are shown below:

function Cube(X: real): real;

begin
    Cube:= (X ∗ X ∗ X);
end;

function Power(X: real; Y: integer): real;

var
    Z: real:

```
begin
    Z:= 1.0;
    while Y > 0 do
        begin
            if odd(Y) then
                Z:= Z * X;
            I:= I div 2;
            x:= sqr(X);
        end;
    Power:= Z;
end;
```

Note that both functions have a statement that assigns a value to the name of the function.

5.2.1   FUNCTION CALL

A function may be called from within an expression. The two examples shown here call the functions Power and Cube:

```
Z2:= Power(X2, Y2);

if Volume = Cube(W) then
    "
    "
    "
```

Like procedures, the number and type of actual parameters must be the same as the number and type of corresponding formal parameters. Functions may be defined within procedures and other functions. Although Pascal permits variable parameters to be passed to functions, it is general practice not to use them. Functions are usually defined as returning a single value. Therefore, if it is necessary to return more than one value, a procedure should be written instead of a function.

5.3 SCOPE OF IDENTIFIERS

The scope of an identifier refers to those parts of the program – known as blocks – in which the identifier is active. A block consists of a definition part, declaration part and statement part.

There are two situations that are considered here regarding the scope of identifiers. First, suppose that two variables, each called Number, are declared in a program and one of its procedures. When the main program has program control, the identifier Number refers to the program variable. When the procedure has program control, the identifier Number refers to the procedure variable.

Now let's consider the more general situation. What is the scope of an identifier when duplicate identifier names have not been declared? The scope of a global identifier – an identifier declared in the main program – is the entire program. The scope of a local identifier is the subprogram in which it is declared along with other subprograms declared within that subprogram. The example on the following page illustrates some possibilities.

TABLE 5.3.1   SCOPE OF IDENTIFIERS

Identifiers defined in:	Their scope is blocks:
Program A	A, B, C, D, E, F
Procedure B	B, C, D
Procedure C	C
Procedure D	D
Procedure E	E, F
Procedure F	F

```
program A
   procedure B
      procedure C
         begin {C}
            "
            "
            "
         end;  {C}
      procedure D
         begin {D}
            "
            "
            "
         end   {D}
      begin {B}
         "
         "
         "
      end;  {B}
   procedure E
      procedure F
         begin {F}
            "
            "
            "
         end   {F}
      begin {E}
         "
         "
         "
      end   {E}
   begin {A}
      "
      "
      "
   end.  {A}
```

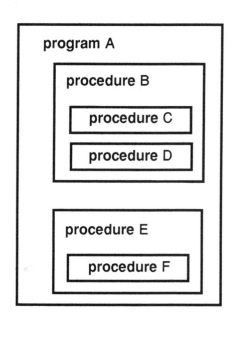

65

5.4 RECURSION

A recursive definition is a definition in which something (i.e. a set or function) is defined in terms of a simpler version of itself. There are two parts to a recursive definition – the basis clause and the general or inductive clause. The basis clause presents the case for which the solution can be stated nonrecursively. The inductive clause presents the case for which the solution is expressed in terms of a simpler version of itself.

In Pascal, recursion is a process whereby a function or procedure references itself. Direct recursion is when a function or procedure invokes itself. Indirect recursion is when a function or procedure invokes another subprogram or series of subprograms which eventually invokes the first subprogram. The following recursive function returns the greatest common factor:

```
function GCF(M, N: NonNegInt): NonNegInt;

begin
   if N = 0 then
      GCF:= M
   else
      GCF:= GCF(N, M mod N);
end;
```

The statement

```
GCF:= M
```

corresponds to the basis clause in a recursive definition, while the statement

```
GCF:= GCF(N, M mod N)
```

corresponds to the inductive clause.

The next recursive function is somewhat more complex. It is known as Ackerman's function:

function Ackerman (M, N: NonNegInt): NonNegInt;

```
begin
    If M = 0 then
        Ackerman:= N + 1
    else if (M <> 0) and (N = 0) then
        Ackerman:= Ackerman(M – 1, 1)
    else
        Ackerman:= Ackerman(M – 1, Ackerman(M, N – 1))
end;
```

Note that in this example there are two statements that make up the inductive clause. The second of these

```
Ackerman:= Ackerman(M – 1, Ackerman(M, N – 1))
```

invokes itself twice. Also note that the second reference to the function Ackerman is actually the second parameter to the first reference.

5.4.1 RECURSIVE CALLS AND THE STACK

Whenever a procedure or function is called recursively, a new set of value parameters and local variables is allocated. Only the new set may be referenced within that call. This set is known as an **activation record**. When a return from the procedure or function takes place, the most recent activation record is freed and the previous copy is reactivated.

Pascal uses a **stack** to keep track of activation records. A stack is a FILO (first-in-last-out) data structure. Whenever a new activation record is activated, it is pushed onto the stack. Whenever an activation record is freed, it is popped off the stack.

Now, what happens when the recursive function GCF presented earlier is first called with M = 196 and N = 36? The series of stack figures in Figure 5.4.1.1 show the changes that take place in the stack contents each time the GCF is invoked. Understanding how Pascal handles the stack with recursive calls will help the reader understand how recursion works.

FIGURE 5.4.1.1 CHANGES IN STACK CONTENTS WHEN GCF
IS INITIALLY INVOKED WITH GCF(196, 36)

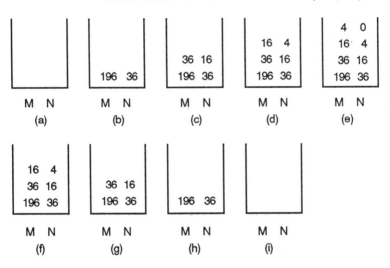

In Figure 5.4.1.1, each row in a stack figure represents an activation record. The current activation record is on top of the stack. When GCF is called for the first time, an activation record is created with M = 196 and N = 36 which is pushed onto the stack (Figure 5.4.1.1.b). Since N <> 0, GCF is called recursively by the statement **GCF:= GCF(N, M mod N)** where N = 36 and (M mod N) = 16. A new activation record is created with M = 36 and N = 16 (Figure 5.4.1.1.c). Keep in mind that the actual parameters are matched up with the formal parameters according to their relative positions. Therefore, the actual parameter N is matched with the formal parameter M, while the actual parameter M mod N is matched with the formal parameter N.

GCF is called again recursively with N = 16 and M mod N = 4 (Figure 5.4.1.1.d) and then with N = 4 and M mod N = 0 (Figure 5.4.1.1.e). Since the value of the formal parameter N in the last activation record is now equal to zero (Figure 5.4.1.1.e), GCF returns a value of 4 with the execution of the statement **GCF:= M**. As a part of this process, an activation record is deallocated and popped off the stack resulting in Figure 5.4.1.1f.

Remember that when GCF called itself recursively with the statement **GCF:= GCF(N, M MOD N)** an activation record was created and the execution of GCF started anew. When an activation record is deallocated and the stack is popped, program execution continues with the statement following **GCF:= GCF(N, M MOD N)**. In this case, the next statement is the **end** statement that terminates the procedure. When the **end** statement is reached, another activation record is deallocated and the stack is popped again. This procedure continues until there are no more activation records and the stack is empty.

In Figure 5.4.1.2, each row in a stack figure represents an activation record. The current activation record is on top of the stack. When Fibonacci is called for the first time an activation record is created with N = 5, and is pushed onto the stack (Figure 5.4.1.2.a). Since N <> 1, Fibonacci is called recursively by the statement **X:= Fibonacci(N – 1)** where N – 1 = 4. A new activation record is created with N now equal to four (Figure 5.4.1.2.b). This process continues until N = 1 (Figure 5.4.1.2.e).

When N = 1, Fibonacci returns a value of 1 for X giving the first Fibonacci number. As a part of this process an activation

FIGURE 5.4.1.2   CHANGES IN STACK CONTENTS WHEN
                 FIBONACCI IS INITIALLY INVOKED WITH A
                 VALUE OF 5.

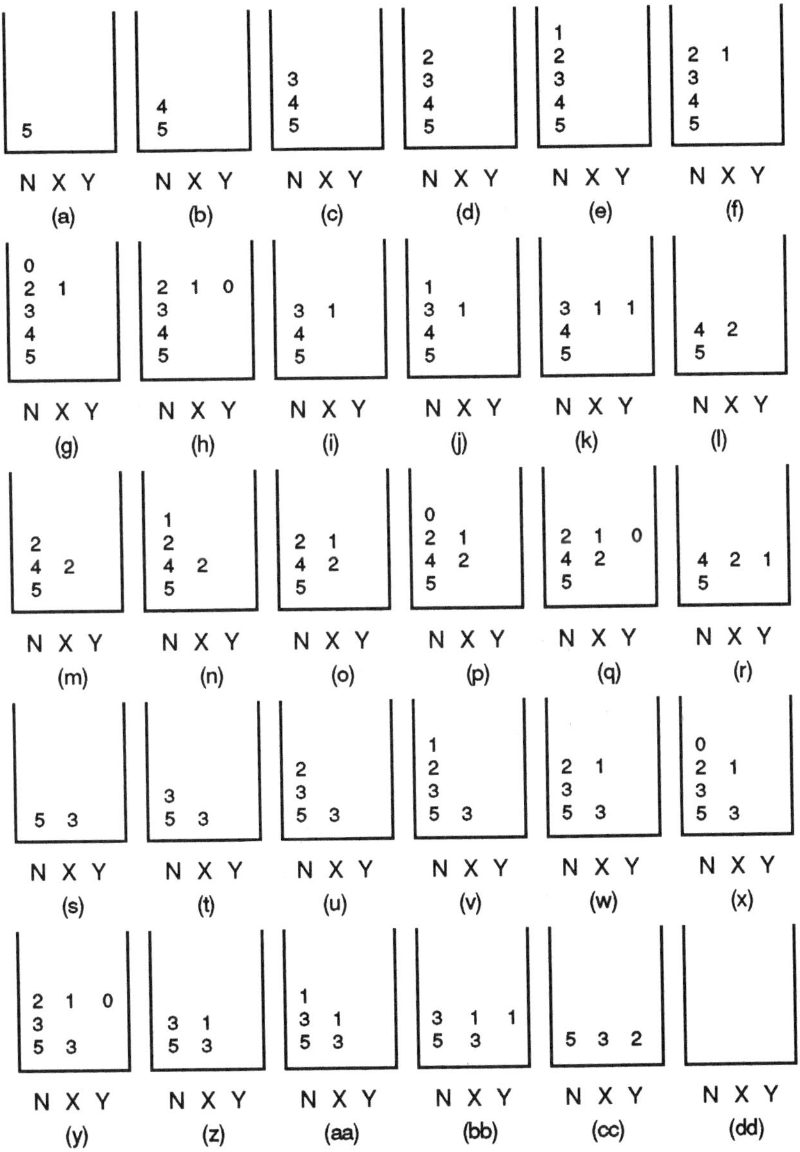

```
|       |    |       |    |       |    |       |    | 1     |    | 2  1  |
|       |    |       |    |       |    | 2     |    | 2     |    | 3     |
|       |    | 4     |    | 3     |    | 3     |    | 3     |    | 4     |
|       |    | 4     |    | 4     |    | 4     |    | 4     |    | 5     |
| 5     |    | 5     |    | 5     |    | 5     |    | 5     |    |       |
 N  X Y       N  X Y       N  X Y       N  X Y       N  X Y       N  X Y
  (a)          (b)          (c)          (d)          (e)          (f)
```

```
| 0     |    |       |    |       |    |       |    |       |    |       |
| 2  1  |    | 2  1 0|    |       |    | 1     |    |       |    |       |
| 3     |    | 3     |    | 3  1  |    | 3  1  |    | 3  1 1|    |       |
| 4     |    | 4     |    | 4     |    | 4     |    | 4     |    | 4  2  |
| 5     |    | 5     |    | 5     |    | 5     |    | 5     |    | 5     |
 N  X Y       N  X Y       N  X Y       N  X Y       N  X Y       N  X Y
  (g)          (h)          (i)          (j)          (k)          (l)
```

```
|       |    | 1     |    |       |    | 0     |    |       |    |       |
| 2     |    | 2     |    | 2  1  |    | 2  1  |    | 2  1 0|    |       |
| 4  2  |    | 4  2  |    | 4  2  |    | 4  2  |    | 4  2  |    | 4  2 1|
| 5     |    | 5     |    | 5     |    | 5     |    | 5     |    | 5     |
 N  X Y       N  X Y       N  X Y       N  X Y       N  X Y       N  X Y
  (m)          (n)          (o)          (p)          (q)          (r)
```

```
|       |    |       |    |       |    | 1     |    |       |    | 0     |
|       |    |       |    | 2     |    | 2     |    | 2  1  |    | 2  1  |
|       |    | 3     |    | 3     |    | 3     |    | 3     |    | 3     |
| 5  3  |    | 5  3  |    | 5  3  |    | 5  3  |    | 5  3  |    | 5  3  |
 N  X Y       N  X Y       N  X Y       N  X Y       N  X Y       N  X Y
  (s)          (t)          (u)          (v)          (w)          (x)
```

```
| 2  1 0|    |       |    | 1     |    |       |    |       |    |       |
| 3     |    | 3  1  |    | 3  1  |    | 3  1 1|    |       |    |       |
| 5  3  |    | 5  3  |    | 5  3  |    | 5  3  |    | 5  3 2|    |       |
 N  X Y       N  X Y       N  X Y       N  X Y       N  X Y       N  X Y
  (y)          (z)          (aa)         (bb)         (cc)         (dd)
```

70

record is deallocated and popped off the stack resulting in Figure 5.4.1.2.f.

At this point, Fibonacci is called by the statement **Y:= Fibonacci(N – 2)**. Since N = 2 in the top activation record, N – 2 = 0 (Figure 5.4.1.2.g). In the new invocation of Fibonacci with N now equal to zero, Fibonacci returns a zero to Y (Figure 5.4.1.2.h).

Now our activation record has a value for X and Y so Fibonacci returns a value of X + Y = 1 + 0 = 1 for the second Fibonacci number. This value is returned to X in the previous activation record (Figure 5.4.1.2.i).

This process continues until Fibonacci returns a 5 for N = 5 (Figure 5.4.1.2.cc: X + Y = 3 + 2 = 5). Note that when Fibonacci returns this value, the stack is empty.

Recursion, when used properly, is a powerful programming tool. In some cases, it can improve performance over iterative algorithms. In other cases, a recursive algorithm may be more natural and easier to understand than its iterative counterpart even if the former is not quite as efficient as the latter. For another example of recursion, the reader is referred to the quicksort procedure in Chapter 6.

5.5   SAMPLE PROGRAM

program PrimeDivisors(Numfile, Primefile);

```
{   This program reads a file of integers and generates their prime   }
{   divisors.                                                          }
```

var
    NumFile, PrimeFile: text;

```pascal
procedure OpenFiles(var NumFile,  PrimeFile: text);

begin { OpenFiles }
    reset(NumFile);
    rewrite(PrimeFile);
end;    { OpenFiles }

procedure CloseFiles(var NumFile,  PrimeFile: text);

begin { CloseFiles }
    close(NumFile);
    close(PrimeFile);
end;    { CloseFiles }

procedure ProcessFile(var NumFile, PrimeFile: text);

var
    Number: integer;

    procedure  FindNextPrimeNumber (var PrimeNumber: integer);

    {   FindNextPrimeNumber receives the current prime  }
    {   number and calculates and returns the next larger  }
    {   prime number.                                      }

    var
        prime:    boolean;
        divisor:  integer;

    begin { FindNextPrimeNumber }
        if PrimeNumber= 2 then
            PrimeNumber:= 3
        else
                begin { else}
                    Prime:= false;
```

```
            while not Prime do
                begin { while }
                    Prime:= true;
                    PrimeNumber:= PrimeNumber + 2;
                    divisor:= 3;
                    repeat
                        if PrimeNumber mod divisor = 0 then
                            Prime:= false;
                        divisor:= divisor + 2;
                    until (not Prime) or
                        (divisor > sqrt(PrimeNumber));
                end;  { while}
            end;  { else }
    end;  { FindNextPrimeNumber }


procedure WritePrime(var PrimeFile: text; Prime Number: integer;
                    var First: boolean);

    begin    { WritePrime }
        if First then
            begin { if }
                write(PrimeFile, PrimeNumber);
                First:= false;
            end{if }
        else
            write(PrimeFile, ' * ' , PrimeNumber);
    end;    { WritePrime }


procedure FindPrimeDivisors(var NumFile, PrimeFile: text;
                        Number: integer);


{   FindPrimeDivisors calculates all of the prime divisors of      }
{   Number including prime divisors which occur more than once.     }
{   This procedure will need to be studied closely in order to be   }
{   fully understood. Some enhancements have been made to           }
{   make it more efficient – albeit, somewhat more difficult to     }
{   understand. The procedure begins by storing the value of        }
{   Number in TempNumber and then setting PrimeNumber to 2.         }
```

```
{  The code in the repeat loop determines whether PrimeNumber is a    }
{  divisor of TempNumber. If so, the PrimeNumber is written to the     }
{  output file and TempNumber is set equal to TempNumber div           }
{  PrimeNumber. This process continues until PrimeNumber >             }
{  sqrt(Number) or TempNumber = 1. Note: This algorithm works if the   }
{  boolean expression in the until statement is comprised of only      }
{  TempNumber = 1, although it is not nearly as efficient for large values }
{  of Number. There is one difficulty, however. If the value of TempNum- }
{  ber is greater than the square root of Number, then TempNumber is a  }
{  prime divisor of Number and needs to be written to the output file.  }
{  Thus the if statement if TempNumber > sqrt(Number) then ... after    }
{  the repeat loop.                                                     }

var
     First: boolean;
     TempNumber, PrimeNumber: integer;

begin    { FindPrimeDivisors }
     TempNumber:= Number;
     write(PrimeFile, TempNumber:5, ' = ');
     PrimeNumber:= 2;
     First:= true;
     repeat
          if TempNumber mod PrimeNumber = 0 then
               begin   { if }
                    TempNumber:= TempNumber div PrimeNumber;
                    WritePrime(PrimeFile, PrimeNumber, First);
               end{ if }
          else
               FindNextPrimeNumber (PrimeNumber);
     until (PrimeNumber > sqrt(Number)) or (TempNumber = 1);
     if TempNumber > sqrt(Number) then
          WritePrime(PrimeFile, TempNumber, First);
     writeln(PrimeFile);
end;    { FindPrimeDivisors }

begin    { ProcessFile }
     while (not eoln(NumFile)) do
          begin   { while }
               read(NumFile, Number);
               if Number <= 1 then
                    writeln(PrimeFile, Number:5,
                    ' is an ILLEGAL number.')
               else
```

```
                FindPrimeDivisors(NumFile, PrimeFile, Number);
        end;    { while }
        readln(NumFile);
end;

procedure WriteEndProgramMessage;

begin
    writeln;
    writeln;
    writeln('>> end program execution');
end;

begin  { main program }
    OpenFiles(NumFile, PrimeFile);
    while (not eof (NumFile)) do
        ProcessFile(NumFile, PrimeFile);
    CloseFiles(NumFile, PrimeFile);
    WriteEndProgramMessage;
end.    { main program }
```

Listed below is an input file to PrimeDivisors and its corresponding output file:

Input File

291	24	821	
7777	89	-2	10111
93	8467		
3993	2	-3343	

Output File

```
  291 = 3 * 97
   24 = 2 * 2 * 2 * 3
  821 = 821
 7777 = 7 * 11 * 101
   89 = 89
   -2 is an ILLEGAL number.
10111 = 10111
   93 = 3 * 31
 8467 = 8467
 3993 = 3 * 11 * 11 * 11
    2 = 2
-3343 is an ILLEGAL number.
```